How Are We Doing? Evaluating Manager and Board Performance

Vaughn Mamlin Upshaw

UNC
SCHOOL OF
GOVERNMENT

The School of Government at the University of North Carolina at Chapel Hill works to improve the lives of North Carolinians by engaging in practical scholarship that helps public officials and citizens understand and improve state and local government. Established in 1931 as the Institute of Government, the School provides educational, advisory, and research services for state and local governments. The School of Government is also home to a nationally ranked graduate program in public administration and specialized centers focused on information technology and environmental finance.

As the largest university-based local government training, advisory, and research organization in the United States, the School of Government offers up to 200 courses, webinars, and specialized conferences for more than 12,000 public officials each year. In addition, faculty members annually publish approximately 50 books, manuals, reports, articles, bulletins, and other print and online content related to state and local government. Each day that the General Assembly is in session, the School produces the *Daily Bulletin Online*, which reports on the day's activities for members of the legislature and others who need to follow the course of legislation.

The Master of Public Administration Program is offered in two formats. The full-time, two-year residential program serves up to 60 students annually. In 2013 the School launched MPA@UNC, an online format designed for working professionals and others seeking flexibility while advancing their careers in public service. The School's MPA program consistently ranks among the best public administration graduate programs in the country, particularly in city management. With courses ranging from public policy analysis to ethics and management, the program educates leaders for local, state, and federal governments and nonprofit organizations.

Operating support for the School of Government's programs and activities comes from many sources, including state appropriations, local government membership dues, private contributions, publication sales, course fees, and service contracts. Visit www.sog.unc.edu or call 919.966.5381 for more information on the School's courses, publications, programs, and services.

Michael R. Smith, Dean
Thomas H. Thornburg, Senior Associate Dean
Frayda S. Bluestein, Associate Dean for Faculty Development
L. Ellen Bradley, Associate Dean for Programs and Marketing
Todd A. Nicolet, Associate Dean for Operations
Bradley G. Volk, Associate Dean for Administration

FACULTY

Whitney Afonso
Trey Allen
Gregory S. Allison
David N. Ammons
Ann M. Anderson
A. Fleming Bell, II
Maureen Berner
Mark F. Botts
Michael Crowell
Leisha DeHart-Davis
Shea Riggsbee Denning
Sara DePasquale

James C. Drennan
Richard D. Ducker
Joseph S. Ferrell
Alyson A. Grine
Norma Houston
Cheryl Daniels Howell
Jeffrey A. Hughes
Willow S. Jacobson
Robert P. Joyce
Kenneth L. Joyner
Diane M. Juffras
Dona G. Lewandowski

Adam Lovelady
James M. Markham
Christopher B. McLaughlin
Kara A. Millonzi
Jill D. Moore
Jonathan Q. Morgan
Ricardo S. Morse
C. Tyler Mulligan
Kimberly L. Nelson
David W. Owens
LaToya B. Powell
William C. Rivenbark

Dale J. Roenigk
John Rubin
Jessica Smith
Meredith Smith
Carl W. Stenberg III
John B. Stephens
Charles Szypszak
Shannon H. Tufts
Vaughn Mamlin Upshaw
Aimee N. Wall
Jeffrey B. Welty
Richard B. Whisnant

Printed in the United States of America

22 21 20 19 18   3 4 5 6 7

ISBN 978-1-56011-742-1

About the Series

Local Government Board Builders offers local elected leaders practical advice on how to effectively lead and govern. Each of the booklets in this series provides a topic overview, and many offer specific tips on effective practice, worksheets, and reflection questions to help local elected leaders improve their work. The series focuses on common activities for local governing boards, such as selecting and appointing committees and advisory boards, planning for the future, making better decisions, improving board accountability, and effectively engaging stakeholders in public decisions.

Vaughn Mamlin Upshaw, lecturer in public administration and government at the UNC School of Government, is the series editor.

Other Books in the Series

Leading Your Governing Board: A Guide for Mayors and County Board Chairs, Vaughn Mamlin Upshaw, 2009

A Model Code of Ethics for North Carolina Local Elected Officials, A. Fleming Bell, II, 2010

Creating and Maintaining Effective Local Government Citizen Advisory Committees, Vaughn Mamlin Upshaw, 2010

Working with Nonprofit Organizations, Margaret Henderson, Lydian Altman, Suzanne Julian, Gordon P. Whitaker, and Eileen R. Youens, 2010

Public Outreach and Participation, John B. Stephens, Ricardo S. Morse, and Kelley T. O'Brien, 2011

Local Government Revenue Sources in North Carolina, Kara A. Millonzi, 2011

Getting the Right Fit: The Governing Board's Role in Hiring a Manager, Vaughn Mamlin Upshaw, John A. Rible IV, and Carl W. Stenberg, 2011

The Property Tax in North Carolina, Christopher B. McLaughlin, 2012

Local Government Budgeting: A Guide for North Carolina Elected Officials, Julie M. Brenman with Gregory S. Allison, 2013

Handbook for North Carolina Mayors and Council Members, David M. Lawrence, 2013

Suggested Rules of Procedure for the Board of County Commissioners, Joseph S. Ferrell, Third Edition 2002

Suggested Rules of Procedure for Small Local Government Boards, A. Fleming Bell, II, Second Edition 1998

Suggested Rules of Procedure for a City Council, A. Fleming Bell, II, Third Edition 2000

Contents

Introduction   1

Linking Levels of Accountability   3

    Questions for Discussion   5

Manager Evaluation   7

    Why should a manager request an evaluation?   7

    Why should a board evaluate the manager?   9

    Questions for Discussion   9

    What constitutes a good performance evaluation process?   10

    How should the manager's performance evaluation be conducted?   10

    Do all manager performance evaluations look alike?   10

    What constitutes a good evaluation instrument?   12

    Should the manager's performance evaluation be standardized?   13

    What can the manager contribute to the evaluation process?   14

    Where can the manager and the board find an example of a performance evaluation instrument?   14

    Questions for Discussion   15

    Who should participate in the manager's performance evaluation process?   15

    Should the board use an external facilitator?   16

    How should a facilitator be chosen?   16

    Questions for Discussion   17

    When should the manager's performance evaluation take place?   17

    Where should the performance evaluation discussion take place?   20

    How long should the performance evaluation discussion last?   20

    Questions for Discussion   21

    What are the major steps in a performance evaluation?   21

        Planning   21

        Instrument Design   23

        Data Collection   24

        Summary Report   26

        Performance Evaluation Discussion   27

        Follow-Up   29

    Questions for Discussion   32

Board Evaluation 33

What is the standard for board accountability? 33

Questions for Discussion 35

Why should the board evaluate itself? 35

What should board members consider before implementing an evaluation? 37

What constitutes an effective board evaluation? 38

Do all board evaluations look alike? 39

Which evaluation instrument should be used? 39

Who should participate in the board's evaluation? 40

What are the steps in board evaluation? 41

When and where should the discussion of the evaluation take place? 42

What type of follow-up is necessary? 42

Questions for Discussion 43

Appendix A: Practices for Effective Local Government Management 45

Appendix B: Sample Board Evaluation Items 53

Appendix C: Governing Board Quick-Scan 63

Introduction

Creating a successful local government requires that the manager and the governing board develop and maintain a culture of mutual respect, trust, and responsibility. The governing board and the public manager are charged with meeting legal, ethical, strategic, financial, and citizen expectations. Together they decide what services will be offered, to whom they will be offered, and what the quality and cost of the services will be. Establishing a set of clear agreements about what the board and manager are responsible for and a system to evaluate both board and manager performance enables a board and its manager to identify areas of strength and opportunities for development.

Even though performance evaluations for city and county managers are voluntary in North Carolina, many governing boards conduct annual evaluations of their managers. Similarly, many governing boards perform self-evaluations not because the law requires it, but because it is best practice. Just as an employee will find it difficult to perform well with unclear expectations and limited feedback on his or her work, a governing board will struggle to operate without agreement on member expectations, roles, and responsibilities. When members of the board have contradictory agendas and struggle to find common ground, or if board members are in conflict, the manager's and the organization's ability to succeed is affected. Professional public managers who work with governing boards that do not agree about priorities and lack professionalism in establishing policies tend to voluntarily leave their positions rather than work in a dysfunctional environment.[1] Public managers and local government experts therefore agree that in addition to conducting performance reviews for the manager, a governing body should review its own performance

---

1. James B. Kaatz, P. Edward French, and Hazel Prentiss-Cooper, "City Council Conflict as a Cause of Psychological Burnout," *State and Local Government Review* 31, no. 3 (Autumn 1999): 162–72. Also see Gordon P. Whitaker and Ruth Hoogland DeHoog, "City Managers under Fire: How Conflict Leads to Turnover," *Public Administration Review* 51, no. 2 (Mar.–Apr. 1991): 156–65.

annually, in conjunction with either its strategic planning retreat or with the manager's evaluation process.[2]

There are many ways for boards to conduct performance evaluations. For a process to be effective, however, it is important to make sure that the approach used is appropriate for the people and circumstances involved. When a clear evaluation process is practiced on a regular basis, it is more likely that the board and manager will build strong, coherent goals for improving performance. Regularly conducting reviews also minimizes the chance that a review will be undertaken only in response to a crisis.

This guidebook describes best practices and offers practical tips for productively evaluating the manager's and the governing board's performance. It provides examples of manager and board evaluation measures, rating scales, and formats along with suggestions for ongoing performance improvement. For those already doing manager or board performance evaluations,[3] this guidebook offers suggestions that can strengthen an existing process. It may also be used as a step-by-step manual for developing a new performance evaluation process from the ground up.

---

2. Gus Morrison and Jan Perkins, "The Value of Going Back to the Basics," *Western City*, June 2005, 7–9. Also see Charldean Newell, "Enhancing the Governing Body's Effectiveness," chap. 3 in *The Effective Local Government Manager* (Washington, D.C.: International City/County Management Association, 2004), 57–82.

3. People use different terms when referring to performance evaluations. Terms such as *performance review*, *annual review*, or *manager evaluation* are used interchangeably and refer to the same thing. In this publication, *performance evaluation* is used to cover all of these alternative terms.

Linking Levels of Accountability

With the passage of the Sarbanes-Oxley Act of 2002,[1] accountability for governing boards in corporate and nonprofit sectors came under increased scrutiny as regulators and stakeholders looked more closely at board financial controls and ethical conduct.[2] North Carolina's public, employees, media, state agencies, and communities also expect city councils and county commissioners to demonstrate responsible financial oversight and ethical standards. Board accountability is an emerging best practice for enhancing governing board performance.

Accountability for the public good occurs through a series of interactions among a variety of partners. A governing board's accountability system should "seamlessly link one level of authority to another,"[3] establishing a shared line of sight for the community, organization, manager, and board (see Figure 1). A comprehensive board accountability system ties the board's expectations for its own performance to expectations in other areas.

Improving accountability is difficult unless performance is monitored across levels in a complementary way. Each level of authority may have well-designed standards for performance, sound measurement systems, and good outcomes, but if expectations across levels are independent of one other, it is not an accountability system. Linking the governing board's accountability system to the one used for evaluating the manager's performance will help the board clarify goals for itself, the manager, and the organization. The governing board's strategic goals guide the public manager's annual priorities, and these priorities are used to establish departmental goals for employees, programs, and resources.

Board accountability systems also help boards and managers clarify how they share responsibility for achieving desired results. Publicly stating expected results and assigning

---

1. Pub. L. No. 107-204, 116 Stat. 745.

2. Megan Rutter Branch, "Newbie's Guide: How to Prep for Your First Board Meeting," *Association Now/The Volunteer Leadership Issue*, January 2008. Also see Cinda Becker, "IRS Affirms Board Accountability," *Modern Healthcare* 37, no. 7 (Feb. 12, 2007): 10.

3. John Carver, "Accountability Isn't Blame: It's a System Characteristic," *Board Leadership* 2007, no. 93 (October 2007): 2.

Figure 1. Creating a Line of Sight for the Board

responsibility for achieving them give elected and appointed officials, as well as the public, ways to monitor and measure change.

It is useful for an annual accountability cycle to be incorporated into the board's calendar. If an outcome is met or exceeded, the board can question whether it needs to adjust performance targets for the next cycle. If an outcome is not met, the board needs to understand why and determine what needs to be done to ensure a better outcome in the next cycle. Figure 2 illustrates a typical board accountability cycle.

Figure 2.   Annual Board Accountability Cycle

1. Set Performance Goals
2. Determine Standards
3. Monitor Results
4. Compare and Evaluate
5. Take Action as Needed

Questions for Discussion

1. What might we do to make our governing board, manager, or organization more accountable?

2. What are the priority areas for a line of sight in our local government?

Manager Evaluation

In North Carolina, all one hundred counties have professional managers, and almost half of the state's cities employ full-time managers.[1] Although North Carolina statutes do not require city councils and boards of county commissioners to evaluate their city and county managers, best practice suggests that governing boards should evaluate their professional managers at least once a year.[2] The majority of city and county managers expect to be evaluated by their elected boards on an annual basis. The following sections focus on assessing the manager's performance.

Why should a manager request an evaluation?

Lack of feedback can cause good managers to perform poorly. Without regular and effective feedback, a manager may believe that he or she is doing what is expected, only to be reprimanded or fired for failing to meet an unstated expectation. Sometimes board members hear about something the manager has done indirectly or secondhand. Such information can cause board members to jump to conclusions about what the manager was doing and why. Without an opportunity to ask the manager directly about what has taken place, the board may perceive the manager as having his or her own agenda. Regular performance evaluations give the manager and board members an opportunity to clarify areas of misunderstanding and establish common goals.

A regular evaluation also allows the board to recognize and reward effective manager performance. It is customary for the governing board to decide whether or not to reward a manager's performance based on a review of his or her work. Without a formal

---

1. In 2013, 46 percent of North Carolina's cites had full-time managers, and 86 percent of cities with populations over 2,000 employed full-time managers. UNC School of Government, Forms of North Carolina City Government database, www.sog.unc.edu/node/427.

2. David N. Ammons and Arnold Rodriguez, "Performance Appraisal Practices for Upper Management in City Governments," *Public Administration Review* 46, no. 5 (Sept.–Oct. 1986): 460–67.

performance evaluation process, the justification for giving the manager a raise or taking other action may be questioned by the manager or the public. If someone asks why the manager was given a raise and the board has little or no justification, it may be difficult to defend the decision.

Some managers will say that they do not need a formal performance evaluation because they are reviewed at every board meeting. Boards, however, rarely engage in conversations about manager performance as part of their regular meetings. Setting aside time for an annual evaluation provides an opportunity for the manager and the board to comprehensively discuss the manager's roles and responsibilities.

Scenario for Discussion

The city manager arrives for his annual performance evaluation feeling good about what he has accomplished over the past year. Following council policies, he maintained services without raising revenues by eliminating unfilled positions; collaborated with the economic development director to recruit a new business that employs 150 people; and gained support from local contractors for a new ordinance that streamlines the approval process for new housing developments.

When the mayor asks the manager to reflect on his performance, the manager replies, "I think I've done well this year." Looking around the room, he notices that the council members are squirming in their chairs and casting sidelong glances at each other. "On no," he says to himself. "What am I missing?"

The mayor clears his throat and asks the council members to state how they think the manager has done. The first member says, "I know you have tried to do a good job this year, but there are still people in my district complaining about the lack of sidewalks and saying that the park needs upkeep." Another member chimes in, "Yes, and I still am waiting for you to respond to my request for a new website that can stimulate additional economic development."

The manager quickly realizes that his evaluation is not going as he anticipated. He says to the council, "I understand that you are frustrated because some of the things you asked for have not been done, but the issues you mentioned were not included in the budget or approved by the full council."

The mayor acknowledges the lack of full council approval on additional budget items but then says, "Citizens are complaining. I think it's time for the council to deliberate. Would you please step out? I will call you back in when we have a decision."

The city manager steps into the hall and takes a deep breath. "This was not what I expected," he mutters to himself. "I may need to start looking for a new job."

Why should a board evaluate the manager?

An annual performance evaluation provides the board and manager a formal opportunity to review the manager's work over the previous year or other specified time period. Professional public managers are responsible for a variety of things, such as carrying out the governing board's directives, managing the local government organization, working with the public, coordinating activities with local business and community groups, and responding to unexpected crises as they occur. When a board and manager take the time to regularly discuss how things are going, the manager is able to offer the board more information about his or her work, and members of the board can make observations, offer advice, and provide feedback in a timely manner.

Conducting regular manager evaluations also allows board members to gain a better understanding of the manager's challenges, particularly those that are outside his or her direct control. Sometimes, board members may think that a manager's inaction on an issue is because the manager is deliberately trying to circumvent the board's directives. In fact, the manager may have encountered unexpected challenges, such as a change in personnel that caused a delay, a regulatory requirement that held up progress on a new development, or an unexpected expense that required shifting resources away from the intended focus. Conducting regular evaluations provides the board and manager the opportunity to address such problems before they become entrenched and hard to correct.

Questions for Discussion

1. What does the manager expect from the evaluation process?
2. What do governing board members expect from the evaluation process?

What constitutes a good performance evaluation process?

A good performance evaluation is designed to provide feedback on a broad range of issues and identify areas of strength and opportunities for development. It should address agreed-upon expectations from the manager's work plans as well as commonly expected standards for professional behavior and character. A performance evaluation process should also have a standard structure and should be applied consistently over time. When performance evaluations are done infrequently, they are more likely to be used as a crisis management tool to address a particular problem rather than as a way of assessing the manager's overall performance.

The performance evaluation should also be designed to provide an opportunity for the board and the manager to discuss options for reviving projects that were not completed. Such a conversation may lead to a revised work plan—perhaps one that puts greater emphasis on the things the manager controls directly or that increases the governing board's responsibility for making sure that the manager has the necessary support and resources to carry out the board's directives.

How should the manager's performance evaluation be conducted?

Although some governing boards delegate the evaluation of the manager to the board chair or mayor or to a subcommittee, the manager works for the entire board and should be evaluated by the full board. In a council–manager or commission–manager form of government, the governing body appoints the manager to serve at its pleasure: thus, the manager is responsible and accountable to the body as a whole.[3] Because individual members of the board may perceive a manager's performance differently, a performance review conducted by one person or by a subcommittee will not reflect the full board's perceptions.

Do all manager performance evaluations look alike?

Performance evaluations come in a variety of shapes and sizes. The critical issue is finding the right approach for a particular situation. Since every manager and organization is unique, and the priorities for communities vary, there is no standard tool that can be used in every situation. There are, however, common features of good performance evaluation instruments that can be tailored to reflect local needs and circumstances.

---

3. North Carolina General Statutes (hereinafter G.S.) §§ 160A-147 (cities and towns) and 153A-76 (counties).

At a minimum, a performance evaluation should be designed to measure the manager's accomplishments during the year. Ideally, the manager and board have a common understanding about what the manager's priorities are and how success in those areas will be measured. If the governing board has not adopted a plan at the beginning of the year, the manager can generate a list of priorities that he or she expects to address in the coming year and ask that the board include these in an evaluation instrument. Without clear priorities, however, the manager's report may generate controversy, because board members may have different ideas about what the manager should do. If the manager's and board's annual goals are unrelated, the manager may receive a positive performance evaluation for accomplishing his or her own goals, only to be fired later on for failing to address the board's priorities.

Scenario for Discussion

A manager operates without a formal work plan, but the governing board has clearly stated that it expects the manager to be responsive, to faithfully carry out board directives, and to operate the local government in an efficient and effective manner. During his evaluation, the manager reports that average response times for citizen requests decreased, several new board policies were implemented, and the local government's financial outlook improved. The board members consider this information sufficient to allow them to fairly evaluate the manager's performance, and they give the manager a high rating.

The performance evaluation may also be designed to measure the manager's performance of routine, ongoing tasks such as communicating with the board, responding to citizens, or improving information technology within the organization. These activities are ones that most public managers are expected to undertake on a regular basis, and they can be measured against agreed-upon standards. However, if the board and manager have not set measurable targets, there can be disagreement among board members or between the board and the manager as to whether or not expectations have been met.

Scenario for Discussion

A town manager has an approved work plan that includes the development of a Unified Development Ordinance (UDO) with the county, the creation of an economic development strategy for a local industrial park, and the implementation of an online permitting process. During the performance evaluation the manager reports that the governing board in the neighboring jurisdiction declined support for the UDO, economic development funding was eliminated from the annual

*budget, and the web developer moved on to a higher-paying job in the private
sector. The board conducts its evaluation and gives the manager a low rating
based on the manager's failure to accomplish the goals set forth in the work plan.*

Professional practices and behaviors that affect the manager's ability to perform well in his or her job are often a part of the performance evaluation as well. This section typically focuses on leadership skills and character traits that are essential to success for any public manager, and managers want and need feedback in this area. Because these traits are subjective and thus more difficult to rate, however, it is important for the board to define terms and set clear measurement standards. How, for instance, do members of the board define "integrity?" What do they mean by "trustworthy," and how can such traits be measured?

Finally, it is important to note that evaluations need to assess not only what has been accomplished, but also how it was accomplished. For example, if a manager develops a consolidated purchasing system but neglects to include the people who will implement it in the planning process, the final system may be inefficient because important stakeholders were not involved from the outset. If the manager is evaluated on having completed the task but not on the way the task was accomplished, he or she may expect a good evaluation, but the board may miss an opportunity to discuss issues critical to the manager's success.

What constitutes a good evaluation instrument?

Once the governing board and manager have agreed upon performance goals and expectations, the board needs to make sure that the evaluation instrument captures these components. A subcommittee of the board and the manager may work together to design an appropriate instrument.

It is important to design an instrument that is easy for the board to complete and yields feedback that the manager can understand. Instruments that have too many items, duplicate questions, or complicated instructions are difficult for board members and often provide confusing and inconsistent feedback to the manager. Since every member of the board is expected to complete the evaluation, all members need to understand the questions and how the responses will be tallied. If members of the governing board cannot answer questions about the manager's performance in an informed manner, they will be frustrated and the evaluation may be incomplete. Incomplete or inaccurate responses are difficult for managers to interpret, and poorly written or ambiguous questions can lead to difficult conversations and conflicting opinions among board members.

Narrowly constructed items can be especially challenging for board members to assess. For example, asking board members to rate the manager's work with specific stakeholder groups or advisory committees may cause governing board members to offer feedback based on hearsay or to be unable to provide a rating because they have no direct knowledge of the manager's performance. If board members are unable to observe behavior and cannot accurately rate performance on an item, it is inappropriate to include that item in an evaluation instrument. Even if the instrument allows board members to indicate that they don't know how to rate the manager in a particular area, members may feel compelled to guess at the manager's competence. An evaluation that is incomplete or based on guesswork is not only unhelpful to the manager but may actually do more harm than good. Generally, if a majority of board members feel that they cannot accurately rate the manager on a particular item, the item should be eliminated from the evaluation instrument.

Occasionally, a manager or board wants to use 360-degree feedback for the manager's evaluation.[4] However, using 360-degree feedback for a managers' performance evaluation is inadvisable for a variety of reasons. Most 360-degree feedback instruments focus on generic leadership and management practices rather than the specific competencies required of a public manager. It is also inappropriate for a mixed group of respondents (including employees who report directly to the manager) to review a manager's performance when the manager works for and is ultimately responsible to the governing board.

Should the manager's performance evaluation be standardized?

A thoughtful performance evaluation process can simultaneously track progress toward annual goals and document ongoing improvement in professional practice. Standardizing sections of a manager's performance evaluation provides information that can be compared over time. Some recurring items, such as preparing an annual budget, can be built into the performance evaluation each year. Other tasks, however, such as putting together a unified development ordinance or a capital improvement plan, may be unlikely to recur annually. Variable items provide feedback on activities that are time-dependent, while stable items offer input on areas associated with ongoing effective management. Varying items on the evaluation to accommodate changes in the manager's annual work plan may be appropriate at times, but changing the entire performance evaluation tool annually makes it difficult to measure the manager's progress.

---

4. For professional management certification, the International City/County Management Association (ICMA) requires managers to complete 360-degree feedback every five years and a performance evaluation every year. The process involves self-evaluation along with feedback from a variety of sources, including the manager's supervisor, employees, and external clients.

What can the manager contribute to the evaluation process?

A city or county manager can begin by providing the board with examples of good performance evaluations. Managers typically know their responsibilities and priorities at work—job descriptions and professional standards detailing the common expectations for public managers are widely available. At the outset of the planning phase, a city or county manager can help the board by preparing a list of priorities that he or she would like to have included in the evaluation. In addition, the manager can identify practices relevant to accomplishing city or county goals. For example, in some areas it may be a priority for the manager to cultivate relationships with local media in order to ensure that the local government's concerns and perspectives are accurately represented. In other areas, the manager's focus may be on working closely with engineers and planners to ensure that infrastructure projects and new developments are designed and implemented in a manner consistent with board policy. In either case, the manager would want his or her priority or focus included the evaluation.

As part of the performance evaluation process, the manager should complete a self-evaluation using the same instrument used by the board. Often the manager's impression of his or her performance will differ from that of the board. Even when the manager and board agree on the major goals for the year, a manager's work usually includes a variety of tasks beyond those identified as important in accomplishing the board's priorities. A manager also may have information about and insight into issues not listed on the annual work plan. When a manager completes a self-evaluation, he or she usually lists achievements in other areas along with priorities accomplished. Many managers also provide a narrative memorandum summarizing overall activities and ongoing challenges. Ideally, the manager's self-evaluation should allow board members to learn both what the manager has accomplished and how he or she feels about the quality of the work.

Where can the manager and the board find an example of a performance evaluation instrument?

The International City/County Management Association (ICMA) has developed a set of practices for effective public management that could be used as a starting point for a performance evaluation instrument. (See Appendix A.) It lists and describes the performance expectations for an effective city or county manager, but it is rare for any one person to be outstanding in every area listed. Depending upon the needs of the jurisdiction, the manager and board could agree on a subset of performance measures—usually five to ten—that they believe are critical for their local government. For instance, in a small jurisdiction where the manager wears many hats, the board and manager might decide that staff development should be a priority for the manager, while a larger organization with a stand-alone human resources department might decide that citizen participation should be a priority.

Questions for Discussion

1. Are the board's expectations for the manager outlined in his or her job description? If so, what are they?
2. What performance expectations need to be evaluated annually?
3. What expectations are variable and need to be evaluated only once or only once every few years?

Who should participate in the manager's performance evaluation process?

Under North Carolina law, the city or county manager works for the entire governing board—not an individual member, mayor or board chair, or subcommittee of the board. Therefore, the manager, the mayor or board chair, and all board members need to participate in the performance evaluation. Depending upon the process agreed upon, there may also be roles for the clerk, city or county attorney, director of human resources, and an external facilitator.

Typically the mayor or board chair assumes a leadership role. This may include initiating the annual evaluation process, helping draft an evaluation instrument, setting forth a process for the manager and board to follow, managing the performance evaluation conversation, and working with the manager on specific issues following the performance evaluation. The mayor or chair can help ensure that a performance evaluation process succeeds by inviting the manager and board members to contribute their ideas about what is important to include in the evaluation. The mayor or chair may work with the manager and a subcommittee or external facilitator on an evaluation instrument that reflects the expectations of both the manager and the board. Because people are often uncomfortable giving and receiving feedback, the mayor or chair can lead by example by setting a positive tone and emphasizing the value of thoughtful performance reviews.

Should the board use an external facilitator?

Someone trained to facilitate performance evaluations can be a great resource to the governing board and the public manager. Conversations surrounding performance evaluations are often difficult both for the individual receiving feedback and for those charged with providing a critique. Most people are unaccustomed to telling other adults what they do or do not like about the person's behavior or performance. Without someone to guide the process and the conversation, an inexperienced board can encounter surprises and challenges that the members may not be prepared to address.

How should a facilitator be chosen?

If the governing board decides to use a facilitator, it should look for someone who has experience working with governing boards and conducting performance evaluations for senior managers. The city or county human resources director may be experienced in administering performance reviews within the organization, but the process used internally for department heads, supervisors, and professional staff necessarily differs from the process for the public manager or chief executive. Most organizations have job descriptions and performance objectives for internal positions that can be used as a basis for performance evaluations. However, public managers, like chief executive officers, often do not have clear-cut job descriptions and performance expectations; instead, their jobs may be outlined in a more general fashion. For example, a performance goal for the public manager might be "responsiveness to citizens," but the manager has substantial discretion in meeting this goal. An experienced facilitator can help design the performance review instrument, work with members of the board and the manager to develop a plan for the session, analyze responses from the board and manager, and prepare a summary report for the performance review session. A facilitator can also help the board and manager articulate performance goals and identify specific outcomes.

In addition to helping craft a meaningful performance evaluation tool, a facilitator can provide the following benefits:

- *Neutrality.* Ideally, an external facilitator is someone who is trusted by both the manager and the governing board to provide fair and unbiased advice to all.
- *Full participation.* Using an external facilitator frees all members of the governing board to fully participate in the evaluation process. Without an external facilitator, the mayor or board chair is charged with running the meeting *and* providing feedback as a member of the governing board. It is hard to do both things well at the same time.

- *Establishment of boundaries.* Usually a facilitator will talk to all involved prior to implementing a performance evaluation process to make sure that all participants agree on goals for the evaluation and to get input on what issues are important to address. A good facilitator can also ensure that members of the governing board and the manager understand what will and will not be a part of the evaluation process. For example, if a board member attempts to use the performance evaluation session to chastise fellow board members for their lack of support on a particular issue, the facilitator should be able to redirect the conversation back to the manager's performance. Similarly, a facilitator can help a manager find positive ways to use the board's feedback instead of getting defensive.

Questions for Discussion

1. Who will provide leadership during the manager's evaluation process? The board chair or mayor? A subcommittee of the board?
2. Will an internal person conduct the evaluation or will an external facilitator be hired?
3. What will be the responsibilities for the parties involved? Who will decide on the evaluation instrument? Who will facilitate the evaluation conversation? Who will gather feedback and prepare a summary report?

When should the manager's performance evaluation take place?

There are a variety of options for when to do performance evaluations. If the organization routinely does annual reviews on employees' anniversary dates, conducting the manager's review on his or her hire date is consistent with how other reviews are done and may reduce confusion for the manager and other personnel responsible for coordinating and documenting the review. Using hire dates for performance evaluations also allows the organization to stagger reviews and avoid having all employee reviews due at once.

Another advantage of using the manager's hire date for his or her annual performance evaluation is that it gives the manager a full year of employment to complete the tasks initially assigned. If the performance evaluation is scheduled at a time other than the hire date, the manager's first review may occur soon after hiring—or it may be postponed for over a year, leaving a new manager without formal feedback for a long time and possibly leading to false assumptions on the part of the manager or the board. For example, the manager might assume that board members are happy with his or her work because the board has not communicated any information to the contrary, while board members might think that the manager has assumed too much authority and is operating independently of the board. A lack of clear expectations and regular feedback can quickly devolve into a situation where good people with good intentions simply misunderstand each other.

Scheduling the evaluation for the manager's hire date can be a problem, however, if the timing is inconsistent with the annual work schedule for the board. A mid-year hire date, for instance, may make it difficult to incorporate the governing board's annual priorities into the manager's work plan. Consider the example of a governing board that holds an annual planning retreat in February each year and hires a new manager in September. At the retreat, the board members discuss their goals for the community and identify priorities for the coming year. The manager has a set of priority tasks to complete during the first year. At the February retreat, however, the manager learns that the board is interested in accomplishing several goals that were not on the list of tasks given to the manager in September. The manager must then determine whether the tasks in the work plan are still the board's priority or if the goals set at the retreat are the ones he or she should address. This situation becomes especially challenging if the manager's performance review in September was positive and then a new board majority was elected in November. The new majority may have very different goals than the previous governing board and may adopt new priorities at the winter retreat. If the manager does not seek additional clarification about his or her responsibilities for accomplishing the new governing board's priorities, the new board may discover when it evaluates the manager's performance that the manager is still tracking priorities established by the previous board.

A second option is to schedule the manager's performance evaluation around the time the board has a regular planning retreat in the winter. If the manager's performance evaluation is completed in advance of the retreat, accomplishments can be documented and ongoing work identified prior to planning for the next year. A benefit of conducting performance evaluations in the late fall or early winter is that the governing board can get an in-depth update on work accomplished since the last strategic planning session and identify priorities that still need attention. Another advantage of a late fall or early winter schedule for performance evaluation is that this is typically a slower time of the year and the manager and board members can take time to be reflective. The budget is in place, any new members of the governing board have been sworn in, and the manager has had enough time to complete major projects.

A disadvantage of linking the manager's performance review to the board's strategic planning cycle, however, is that the board may become focused on the manager's work plan rather than on the board's priorities for the future of the community. If the board begins to look at the manager's performance evaluation as the only way to benchmark its own accomplishments, there is a danger of the manager's work plan becoming the board's strategic plan. Of course, the manager is responsible for implementing the board's policy priorities in a given year—but the board's priorities should be more ambitious and comprehensive than the manager's work plan. If the manager's performance evaluation is used as the major source of feedback on the board's strategic plan, the board misses the opportunity to assess its own progress and reflect on what it has or has not done to accomplish its own goals.

A third option is to conduct the manager's performance evaluation in advance of approving the budget. This enables the board to decide whether or not to include a raise for the manager in the annual budget. If the manager accomplished the goals on his or her work plan, the governing board may use these accomplishments to justify a raise. Similarly, if the manager failed to complete agreed-upon goals, the governing board has a justifiable reason not to give the manager raise. The latter example could also provide the board with a legitimate reason to let a poorly performing manager go.

Another obvious benefit of tying the manager's performance evaluation to the budget cycle is that it allows the board to allocate resources accordingly. If the local governing board is operating with a tight budget, governing board members are unlikely to support putting additional money in the manager's salary line "just in case" he or she has a good performance evaluation. Conducting the performance evaluation before the budget is approved prevents the board from having to estimate how much money it may need to allocate for the manager's salary.

The downside of linking the budget cycle and the performance evaluation is that the conversation may be influenced by monetary incentives. Performance evaluation has an inherent value apart from financial reward, and linking the two often diminishes the focus on the intrinsic value of the manager's work. Most public servants have chosen their work because they care about their communities, not because they think they are going to make a lot of money. If the public manager's performance evaluation is conducted in conjunction with the budget cycle, the governing board and the public may begin to think that the only reason the manager is undergoing a performance evaluation is to get a raise. Disentangling the performance evaluation from the budgeting process can reduce the perception that the performance evaluation is primarily designed to decide levels of compensation.

In summary, there is no single answer to the question of when the manager's performance should take place. Each local government should consider the pros and cons discussed above and make a decision based on its own unique circumstances.

Where should the performance evaluation discussion take place?

The location selected for the performance evaluation can influence its outcome. Although it may be convenient to conduct the manager's performance evaluation in the regular council chamber (or another room regularly used for closed sessions), these environments are associated with formal activities and may create unintended tension, especially if members of the board are all on one side of the table and the manager is on the other side. Even when people sit around a table, they are likely to sit in their regular seats, thus reinforcing formal roles and relationships.

As a best practice, individuals participating in the performance evaluation should gather in a neutral space, thereby reducing the chance that people will sit in their customary seats and play traditional roles.[5] Most local governments have conference rooms or can gain access to other public meeting spaces nearby. The board chair or mayor should do his or her best to avoid having people sit as they normally would in a board meeting. If possible, people should sit around the room or around a table facing one another. The manager should be seated in the same way that the members of the governing board are in order to emphasize the fact that the manager, too, has an important voice in the performance evaluation process.

How long should the performance evaluation discussion last?

Performance evaluation is an important event for a manager, and even though board members may not have the same level of interest, they should still make every attempt to provide the manager with worthwhile feedback. To allow sufficient time for feedback and discussion, the governing board and manager should plan on the performance evaluation discussion lasting least two hours. In some instances, they may not need all of the time, but it is better to be prepared for in-depth conversation and have the time available than to find that people have to leave before the discussion can be completed.

Ideally, a governing board and manager will set aside time for a stand-alone session expressly for performance evaluation rather than tack it onto the end of a regular board meeting. If at all possible, it is advisable that the governing board avoid doing the manager's

---

5. Brian Gunia and Brice Corgnet, "Did I Do That? Group Positioning and Asymmetry in Attributional Bias," paper presented at IACM 23rd Annual Conference (2010), available at http://papers.ssrn.com/sol3/papers.cfm?abstract_id=1612508. Also see Westside Toastmasters, "Seating Arrangements—Where to Sit and Why," chap. 17 in *Dimensions of Body Language*, available at http://westsidetoastmasters.com/resources/book_of_body_language/toc.html.

performance evaluation at the end of a regular meeting when members of the board and the manager are tired and ready to go home. If governing board meetings are held in the evenings, people will have worked a full day and then attended a board meeting, and it may be difficult for them to give the manager's evaluation their full attention. They may also be tempted to rush through the process.

A stand-alone session for performance evaluation still needs to be announced as a public meeting of the board, but once the governing board convenes, it immediately goes into closed session for the purpose of discussing personnel. In this way, the public is aware that the governing board and manager are taking time to discuss performance, but the conversation itself is protected from public view.

Questions for Discussion

1. When and how often will the manager's performance evaluation take place? What is the rationale for doing the performance evaluation at a specific time?

2. Has sufficient time been set aside for the performance review? Is the time convenient for all participants?

3. Will the selected location be conducive to a productive conversation? Can seating be arranged so that everyone can see each other?

What are the major steps in a performance evaluation?

A good performance evaluation is one where the governing board and manager agree on all of the steps in the process. Table 1 provides an overview of the key steps in a performance evaluation: planning, selecting or developing an instrument, gathering data, preparing a summary report, conducting the performance review, and following up. Each of these steps is discussed in more detail in the following sections.

Planning

The first step is for the governing board and the manager to plan the performance evaluation. When a performance evaluation comes as a surprise to the members of the governing board, there is a good chance that some of the individuals who need to participate will be unavailable. Furthermore, if the performance evaluation process does not have support

Table 1. Key Steps and Activities for Effective Performance Evaluations

Process Step	Description	Major Activities
Planning	Determine when and where the evaluation will occur and who will participate.	• Agree on who will participate. • Decide date and time for evaluation (ensure that sufficient time is set aside). • Reserve location for evaluation conversation.
Instrument Design	Decide what to evaluate and how performance will be rated.	• Select measures for performance evaluation (five to seven critical areas). • Determine scale and clearly define what each rating means. • Decide means of distribution. • Assign responsibility for data collection and compilation of summary ratings.
Data Collection	Decide how and by whom information will be collected.	• Distribute assessment as hard and/or electronic copy; provide firm deadline. • Follow up with nonresponders prior to deadline. • Prepare data sheet of individual board member and manager results.
Summary Report	Compute averages and ranges of board responses for each question; prepare summary data report and compile written responses.	• Determine number of responses for each question. • Compute an average board rating for each item. • Determine range of board ratings for each item. • Prepare summary report showing board average, range, and manager rating (if applicable). • Compile written feedback.
Performance Review	Facilitate conversation regarding manager's performance among members of the board and manager.	• Agree upon ground rules for the performance review. • Review rating scale. • Discuss items in performance evaluation focusing on how to improve performance and/or reduce differences in perceptions. Provide specific examples of problems and suggest actions that would be more effective.
Follow-Up	Identify areas for improvement and propose performance-improvement objectives for the coming cycle.	• Do a gap analysis. • Develop performance plan for developmental goals. • Create goals and performance expectations for upcoming cycle.

from everyone involved, there may be resentment and a lack of commitment to the process. It is advisable to reach agreement on the following relatively straightforward issues early on:

- When will the performance evaluation take place?
- Where will the performance evaluation be held?
- Who will participate in the performance evaluation process?

Instrument Design

Once the manager and board have agreed on when the performance evaluation will be conducted, and by whom, the next step is to design the performance evaluation instrument. The following issues need to be decided:

- Will the governing board and manager modify another performance evaluation instrument to fit their specific needs?
- Will the governing board create a performance evaluation instrument by using the manager's job description or annual work plan as the basis for review?

If another performance evaluation instrument is used as a starting point, the board and manager should agree on what items are or are not appropriate for the manager's review. For example, it may be tempting to start with the performance evaluation tool used to assess department heads within the organization. However, the level of expertise and breadth of oversight the governing board expects of the manager typically will not be reflected in an instrument for department heads. Department heads usually are responsible for a set of specific functions within their units, while a manager is usually expected to provide direction and oversight for the entire organization. The performance evaluation instrument for the manager should focus on expected outcomes for the organization and not on the particular manner in which the manager conforms to organizational rules. If specific performance problems are a concern for the governing board, it is best to address them as they happen rather than wait for the manager's formal performance evaluation.

The International City/County Management Association's website provides several examples of specific performance items and instrument formats that managers and boards may borrow or adapt to meet their needs.[6] It is important to remember, however, that a good performance evaluation always reflects the unique requirements of a particular manager serving a particular board. An instrument from another organization is unlikely to match all of those requirements.

---

6. These performance appraisals can be found on the ICMA website at http://icma.org/en/icma/knowledge_network/topics/kn/Topic/197/%20Performance_Appraisals.

The board and manager also need to agree on the rating scale to be used in the performance evaluation process (see the sidebar, Sample Performance Measure and Rating Scales, for examples). A common system for rating performance is "below expectations," "meets expectations," and "exceeds expectations" (this approach assumes that the governing board and manager have established clear expectations prior to implementing the performance evaluation). Another common scale for performance reviews is a Likert Scale, where numbers from one to four or one to five are used to indicate a range from "strongly disagree" (the lowest number) to "strongly agree" (the highest number). If an even-numbered scale is used, raters will be forced to indicate whether they agree or disagree, because there is no mid-point for a neutral rating. An odd-numbered scale allows raters to be undecided or neutral on a given question (for example, by choosing three on a scale from one to five). A performance evaluation that comes back with a lot of undecided or neutral responses offers little guidance on how to improve performance. For that reason, it may be best to design an instrument that allows for more communication between the board and the manager.

Another choice in the design of a performance evaluation instrument is whether the instrument will be available online or administered in hard copy. An online survey is easier to administer and maintains confidentiality for respondents. Another advantage of an online tool is that individual responses are recorded directly into the system, which eliminates the potential for human error in entering the responses. Most online tools provide space for people to add open-ended comments in addition to the numeric ratings. There are a number of online survey services that can be used to create a performance evaluation tool that every member of the governing board and the manager can use.

If members of the governing board are uncomfortable using an electronic survey, the clerk or facilitator can distribute hard copies of the performance evaluation instrument to every member of the governing board. If hard copies are used, extreme care should be taken to assure that the raw feedback is given only to the person designated to summarize the individual responses. Confidentiality for members of the governing board is harder to guarantee with a hard-copy survey. Clear instructions need to be included so that governing board members and the manager understand how the performance evaluation instruments will be collected and summarized.

Data Collection

Everyone participating in the performance evaluation should clearly understand how to complete the instrument, what will be done to assure confidentiality, and who will compile results. If individuals are unclear about how to complete the instrument, they are likely to submit an incomplete or inaccurate review. For example, if the instrument asks people to rate performance using a five-point Likert Scale, but the scale is not clearly labeled, some

Sample Performance Measure and Rating Scales

Read the performance measure "Budgeting and Financial Management" below and then review the different rating scales. What are the advantages and disadvantages of the different scales?

Budgeting and Financial Management: Preparing and administering the budget as well as interpreting financial information to assess the short-term and long-term fiscal condition of the community, determining the cost-effectiveness of programs, and comparing alternative strategies.

Sample 3-point scale:

☐ Needs Improvement   ☐ Meets Expectations   ☐ Exceeds Expectations

(*Note*: This rating scale would translate into "1, 2, 3" for purposes of a summary rating.)

Sample 4-point scale:

1=Never   2=Sometimes   3=Often   4=Always   X=Unable to Rate

(*Note*: This scale has no mid-point or "neutral" option, forcing people to express an opinion.)

Sample 5-point scale:

```
-----------1--------------------2--------------------3--------------------4--------------------5--------------------X--------
```
| Does Not Meet Expectations | Meets Expectations | Exceeds Expectations | Unable to Rate |

(*Note*: Any items with an "X" or "unable to rate" should be left out of the board's summary rating—if a majority of board members cannot rate the item, then no average should be created and/or the item should be dropped from the summary.)

Sample 10-point scale:

Rate from 1–10, 10 being excellent   1   2   3   4   5   6   7   8   9   10

(*Note*: A 10-point scale gives raters more flexibility when deciding upon a rating, but may not lead to clearer results. What would be the difference, for instance, between an average rating of 7.25 and an average rating of 7.75?)

Sample Anchored Scale:

Fails to use controls to influence efficiency or cost effectiveness. Consistently shows significant budget variances without acceptable justifications. Often wastes resources by not carefully reviewing impact of decisions. Fails to follow up when resources are not properly utilized.	Ineffective
Utilizes available controls and procedures to monitor resource utilization effectively and devises appropriate and timely corrective actions as necessary. Efficiently uses resources by evaluating alternatives, selecting appropriate strategies, and implementing best allocation of resources. Budget variances are within acceptable limits.	Moderately Effective / Effective
Develops and implements innovative methods to enhance effectiveness in planning, monitoring, and controlling resources. Aggressively seeks out methods to enhance efficiency and cost reduction. Implements innovative and productive means to stretch and supplement resources while enhancing operations and services. Incorporates comprehensive analyses of financial impact in decision-making process.	Highly Effective / Exceptionally Effective

(*Note*: An anchored scale uses the same rating system for each item, but the statements describing what each rating means will link to the item being rated. This is the most sophisticated system and assures that every person's rating is based on a shared understanding of what the score means. However, developing an anchored scale can be costly and time-consuming.)

people may think that one is the highest rating while others think it is five. A well-designed performance evaluation instrument will include written as well as verbal instructions.

Everyone participating in the performance evaluation should also have sufficient time to complete the form. There is no fixed rule for how much time to allow. The board members and manager need enough time to be thoughtful in completing the evaluation, but if too much lead time is provided, the task may be set aside for more pressing priorities and people may forget to complete it. Usually, a two-week window is long enough for people to find time to complete the performance evaluation, but not so long that it is forgotten.

Summary Report

Once the performance evaluation forms have been completed, a summary report must be prepared. The summary should include, at a minimum, the following information:

- actual number of responses for each question,
- average board rating for each question,
- range of board ratings for each item.

(See the sidebar on average rating and range.)

If the evaluation tool offers a space for raters to make written comments on each item or an overall comment at the end, the comments can be incorporated into the numeric report for each item or provided as an attachment to the summary report.

For an evaluation to be considered and a summary report prepared, a majority of board members should have completed the instrument. Ideally, every member of the governing board will take the time to complete the performance evaluation instrument. Sometimes, one member will not complete the evaluation because of time constraints or because he or she is satisfied with the manager's performance and does not believe that it is important to communicate with the manager through the performance evaluation instrument. Although it is best to have everyone's input, the manager works for the governing board as a whole, and if a majority of board members have completed the performance evaluation, it is better to move forward than to hold up the process. If a majority of board members fail to complete the evaluation, the mayor or board chair should revisit how to proceed.

When summarizing the results of the performance evaluation, it is important to indicate the number of people who responded to each item. Ratings by individual members of the

> ### Average Rating and Range
>
> The *average rating* for each item is computed by dividing the sum of the board member ratings by the number of responses for that question (for example, if four members of a five-member board gave the manager a total rating of 15 points, the average score would be 15 divided by 4, or 3.75). The *range* is simply the lowest and highest of the board ratings for each item (for example, if an item was rated by two board members as a 1, by one board member as a 2, and by another board member as a 3, the range would be 1:3).

board, however, should not appear in the report. The summary evaluation should reflect only a single score for the board. During the meeting to review the manager's performance, individuals are free to offer verbal examples and give praise or criticism, but the summary evaluation should reflect the board's average ratings and the majority recommendations. Note, however, that both the individual members' responses and the summary should be placed in the manager's personnel file.[7]

The amount of time needed to prepare the summary report will vary depending upon the nature of the performance evaluation and the manner in which it was presented. The report for an online evaluation can usually be prepared quickly because the data have already been entered and need only be consolidated and formatted. If the evaluation was done on paper, the person summarizing the results will have to type each response into a single document, which can be time-consuming.

If the manager has completed a self-evaluation, it may be provided as a separate document or it may be included with the summary of board member responses. The manager and board need to use the same assessment instrument. In a combined report, the results should be presented in such a way that everyone can easily see where the manager and board agree and which areas need additional attention.

Performance Evaluation Discussion

Once the summary report has been prepared, the board must schedule a session to discuss the manager's evaluation. It is helpful to set ground rules for this discussion so that the manager and board members agree on how they will conduct themselves. The board may wish to follow the sample ground rules for effective groups set forth in the sidebar on pages 30–31.

The discussion should focus on important issues, and it will be more productive if people provide specific, constructive feedback. This includes giving examples of what went wrong and why it was a problem and offering suggestions for what might work better or be more effective.

Usually, the board and manager will agree that the manager's performance is good in certain areas and needs improvement in others. It is important to acknowledge outstanding performance, but if the conversation focuses only on those things that are going well, the manager and board may miss an opportunity to identify performance problems and ways to improve. The conversation needs to include time for discussion of areas where both the board and the manager agreed there were performance concerns and areas where the manager's perception was high and the board's average perception was low. Figure 3 illustrates feedback opportunities that can result from different ratings by the board and the manager.

---

7. G.S. 160A-168(a).

Figure 3. High-Low Combinations of Manager and Board Performance Ratings

Board Average Rating

	Low	High
High	High-Low Blind Spot	High-High Star Performer
Low	Low-Low Developmental Opportunity	Low-High Hidden Strength

Manager Self-Rating

The performance evaluation discussion can be structured in a variety of ways. In some instances, members of the governing board meet beforehand to review their combined ratings of the manager and clarify what feedback they want to provide and who will provide it. In other cases, the board members and manager meet collectively, with members of the board providing individual feedback to the manager in turn. Regardless of the exact approach, the feedback from the board to the manager needs to balance input from individual members with input from the board as a whole. If board members have met beforehand, individual members will have had a chance to air their individual concerns before discussing an agreed-upon common set of issues with the manager. This approach allows the board to give the manager comprehensive feedback. If, instead, the manager receives feedback directly from each member of the governing board, care should be taken to ensure that any future actions on the part of the manager are endorsed by the majority of the board and not based on individual board member feedback during the performance evaluation session.

It is important to remember that listening is a vital aspect of an effective performance review. Not only does the manager need to listen carefully to the board members' feedback, but the governing board members also need to allow time to listen to the manager in order to understand why some expectations may not have been met. Most professional managers will do their best to accomplish goals, but factors outside of the manager's control can impede or derail progress toward stated objectives. Funding cuts, new regulations, unexpected crises, changes in board priorities, and employee turnover, for example, can interfere with a manager's overall work plan. Unless the manager and board revised the manager's annual work plan during the year to accommodate unexpected changes, the manager's evaluation may end up being based on goals that were, in fact, unachievable. If this is the case, the evaluation instrument and process will need to be redesigned to adapt to new realities.

It is also important for the board and manager to remain focused on the areas being evaluated. If members of the governing board or the manager bring up issues that are unrelated to the specific objectives for the performance review, the manager or the board members themselves may be caught off guard. What if one of the objectives was for the manager to develop a capital improvement plan, and during the evaluation, a board member criticizes the manager for failing to establish a contract for building a new water treatment plant? If the board's expectation was for the manager to have a *plan* for capital improvement—not to *contract* for specific projects—the board member's criticism is not relevant to the manager's evaluation.

Finally, board members should keep in mind that people respond better to praise than to criticism. The performance review and subsequent follow up will be more productive if board members provide feedback on how the manager can be more successful rather than emphasize things that went wrong.

Follow-Up

After the evaluation, the board and manager need to ask the following questions:

- What are the consequences for the manager after the performance evaluation?
- What steps will the manager and the board take to ensure that issues will be addressed?
- How will the board and the manager evaluate progress along the way?

Sample Ground Rules for Effective Groups (with Illustrative Examples)

Test hidden assumptions and intentions

I'm thinking you are concerned about _____. Is this right?

What I understood was _____. What did you understand?

My interest was _____. I did not intend to make things more difficult. Can you tell me what I've done or said that I may not be aware of?

Share important information

When you say _____, it sounds as if you may have more information. Can you share what you've heard?

What relevant information are we missing?

Let's not get bogged down in the details. What do you see as the strategic benefits or costs associated with _____?

Ensure that everyone participates, no one dominates

We haven't heard what you think about this issue. Do you have something to add?

You have made that point clearly. What do others have to say about this?

I'm guessing your experience was different from mine. What can you tell us about how you and your community have been affected?

Use specific examples and agree on what important words mean

Can you give me an example of how this situation has directly affected you?

Can you help me understand from your perspective how this would work?

Can you walk us through your thinking on this?

Explain your reasoning and intent

Can you help me understand how you reached that conclusion? I'm not following your reasoning.

I'd like to share the things I thought were important for this decision. Can you give me feedback on my thought process?

We have a commitment to transparency, right? Can you help me understand why and how this decision was made and how it is in keeping with our core values?

Focus on interests, not positions

What do you need and how does this approach meet your goals?

What concerns do you have that will not be addressed by this approach?

What would a successful resolution of this issue look like to you?

Advocate for your ideas and be curious about those of others

It seems as though you have a preference on this issue. Can you explain what you want to do and why?

I think we should _____. What do you think?

What I saw was _____. Did I miss something?

Sources: Roger Fisher and Daniel Shapiro, *Beyond Reason* (London: Penguin, 2005); Roger Schwarz et al., *The Skilled Facilitator Fieldbook* (San Francisco: Jossey-Bass, 2005); UNC School of Government, *"An Effective Council (Operating Principles),"* www.sog.unc.edu/sites/www.sog.unc.edu/files/An%20Effective%20Council.pdf.

Show appreciation for others' points of view

Can you help me understand how you see things?

Of all the things we have discussed, what do you see as most important?

You have a lot of history in this community. What do you think people will say about this?

Jointly design next steps and individual freedom to choose

Let me offer a possible approach to _____. What do you think of this?

It seems to me we need to take the next step. What options do you think we have?

What issues do we need to decide as a group, and what can individuals decide on their own?

Discuss difficult issues

I realize others want to make a decision quickly, but I'm not sure we have heard from everyone who will be affected. I don't want to put anyone on the spot, but I want to make sure our decision reflects everyone's interest. How do others feel about our asking more questions before we make a final decision?

I get the feeling people may be reluctant to make a decision right now. It is a high-risk situation, but failing to act also has consequences. Before we make a decision, can we take a moment to talk about what we are afraid might happen?

Use a decision-making approach that allows for informed decisions and generates commitment

This is a decision I want us to be in agreement about. Can we test to see if we have consensus and commitment before moving forward? If we are not in agreement, we will need to have a special meeting to work out differences before the next regular meeting. What do others think about this approach?

This is a big issue and we will need to have strong support for it to succeed. Before calling for a vote, can we check to see if everyone is prepared to act? If people are not yet ready to decide, can we make a list of questions or concerns we need to address before taking the next step?

We need to take a long-term view and honestly assess our positives and negatives. How will we know if our current approaches are/are not working?

Find merit in others' points of view

Even though I disagree with your conclusion, I see the value in your point of view.

I think it makes sense that you don't want to be excluded from the negotiation.

I appreciate what you have done to make this work.

Be fair and consistent in making decisions, no matter who is affected

We are committed to hearing from all parties affected by our decisions. Have we done that in this case?

My understanding is that we have a local policy to provide guidance in situations like this. Why are we making an exception in this case?

Historically, we have given everyone the same opportunity to _____. Can you help me understand why our approach won't work for this person or group?

Questions for Discussion

It may be helpful to do a gap analysis of the goals for the manager's performance and how well the manager achieved those goals. The board should ask the following questions:

1. If few goals were met, was it because the goals were too high to begin with?
2. Were goals not met due to circumstances outside the manager's control?
3. Were goals not met because members of the board kept changing their expectations during the year?
4. If goals were exceeded, were the goals not set high enough?
5. Did the manager really go above and beyond the call of duty?
6. Should the board set more ambitious goals for the next cycle?

Board Evaluation

People with power are expected to assume responsibility as a part of their authority, and public officials are expected to be answerable to the elected legislature or the electorate. It is unrealistic for the public to hold local elected officials accountable for each thing local government does, but it is reasonable to expect a governing board to set and monitor goals for local government.[1] The governing board is ultimately accountable for organizational activity and accomplishment.[2] To fulfill their accountability role, elected officials need to understand what they are accountable for, recognize how their performance affects other parts of the organization, and identify ways to obtain feedback and improve their oversight role.

Conscientious elected officials want to do a good job for their community and their local government, and they want to know that they are representing themselves and their communities well. Governing board members "must take it upon themselves to look critically at their individual and collective roles and seek to make constructive changes."[3] The following sections focus on assessing the governing board's performance.

What is the standard for board accountability?

There is no single standard for board accountability. City and county elected officials are held accountable for different things in different ways. For instance, city councils and boards of county commissioners are responsible for (1) following local, state, and federal laws; (2) working with others on the board, in government, and in the community; (3) setting

---

1. Carolyn Oliver, "Board Accountability in Highly Constrained Environments," *Board Leadership* 2005, no. 80 (July–August 2005): 2–5.

2. John Carver, *Boards That Make a Difference: A New Design for Leadership in Nonprofit and Public Organizations* (San Francisco: Jossey-Bass, 1997), 2. Also see J. E. Pynes, *Human Resources Management for Public and Nonprofit Organizations* (San Francisco: Jossey-Bass, 1997).

3. James H. Svara, "Contributions of the City Council to Effective Governance," *Popular Government* 51, no. 4 (Spring 1986): 5.

Figure 4. Essential Responsibilities of Local Governing Boards

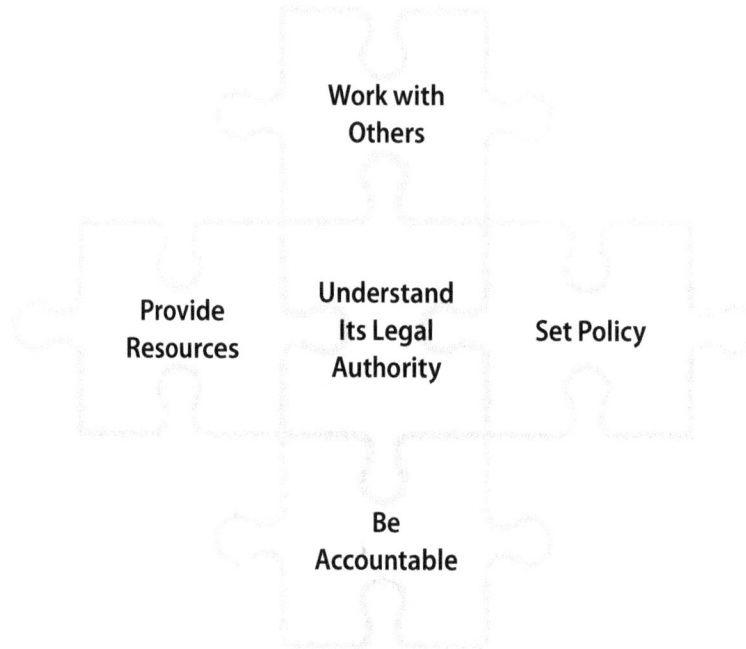

Work with
Others

Provide
Resources

Understand
Its Legal
Authority

Set Policy

Be
Accountable

direction and making policy; (4) overseeing local government finances; and (5) making sure the local government is accountable (see Figure 4). Board members also are required to adopt and abide by a code of ethics.[4] Exactly what specific local elected officials are responsible for in each of these areas differs, as do the penalties for failure. Board members should annually agree upon what the local board is responsible for in each of these areas, what performance standards they will use to accomplish shared work, and how they will hold themselves accountable for meeting these expectations.

At a minimum, a public governing board's goals should include at least one item in each of the following areas:

- operating within the board's legal authority and carrying out both policymaking and adjudicatory duties with obedience, care, and loyalty;
- building effective teams by working well as a board and with the public manager and other professional staff;

---

4. North Carolina General Statutes § 160A-86. Also see Fleming A. Bell, II, *A Model Code of Ethics for North Carolina Local Elected Officials* (Chapel Hill, N.C.: UNC School of Government, 2010).

- engaging citizens and organizational partners in fulfilling the organization's mission and purpose;
- planning strategically for the community's future by determining what programs and services will be provided to whom and at what level of quality;
- ensuring that resources are adequate and effectively managed to provide services;
- supporting the manager and reviewing his or her performance and the board's performance in order to provide oversight for resources, programs, and services.[5]

Questions for Discussion

1. What does accountability mean for me in my present role?
2. What do I hold the board, manager, and organization accountable for?
3. What do I know now about accountability that I wish I had known when I was newly elected?
4. What can be done to make our governing board, manager, or organization more accountable?

Why should the board evaluate itself?

There is growing evidence that organizational effectiveness is associated with governing boards that perform effectively.[6] While most of the research on board effectiveness has been done in corporate and nonprofit arenas, many of these lessons are relevant to public governing boards and managers. Private, public, and nonprofit governing boards are all responsible for things such as overseeing resources, selecting and evaluating the chief executive or manager, monitoring programs and services, and providing strategic direction

---

5. Richard T. Ingram, *Ten Basic Responsibilities of Nonprofit Boards* (Washington, D.C.: National Center for Nonprofit Boards, 2008). Also see Vaughn Mamlin Upshaw, "Essential Responsibilities of Local Governing Boards," *Popular Government* 71, no. 2 (Winter 2006): 14–25.

6. Robert D. Herman and David O. Renz, "Board Practices of Especially Effective and Less Effective Local Nonprofit Organizations," *American Review of Public Administration* 30, no. 2 (June 2000): 146–60. The survey instrument measured mission definition and review, CEO selection and review, working relationship between board and CEO, program selection consistent with mission and program monitoring, giving and soliciting contributions, financial management, strategic planning, new board member selection and training, working relationships between board and staff, marketing and public relations, conduct of board and committee meetings, and role in risk management.

for their organizations. Research on effective governance indicates that boards involved in setting strategy for their organizations and boards with members who work well interpersonally create more value for their organizations than boards that do not perform well in these areas.[7]

Conscientious elected officials want to do a good job for their communities and for their local governments, and they want to know that they are representing themselves and their communities well. Governing board members must therefore "take it upon themselves to look critically at their individual and collective roles and seek to make constructive changes."[8] Elected officials committed to good government will benefit from board evaluation because it enables them to improve the effectiveness, efficiency, and accountability of the governing board and the local government.

Scenario for Discussion

After a hard-fought campaign for city council, a new member walks into the city hall excited about attending her first meeting as a member of the board. As she approaches the meeting room, she stops to listen to a conversation between two members just inside the doorway. "What are we going to do?" one person says. "There is no way she's going to support our proposal to cut funding for public works." The other person responds, "She doesn't have to know we are proposing a cut. As far as she knows, funding is going to be at the same level as it was last year. What she doesn't know won't hurt her."

Taking a deep breath, the new member steps into the room and nods at the two men standing nearby. The men quickly look away, take their seats, and start shuffling papers. Looking over the agenda for the meeting, the new member sees an item on the consent agenda to change the schedule for sidewalk improvements. She considers what she overheard and wonders if the public works budget will be cut if the sidewalk project is postponed. She knows that some of the neighborhoods in her district have been waiting for years for the city to put in sidewalks. "I can't allow this to be put off," she thinks to herself.

The mayor calls the meeting to order. There is a quick motion and vote to approve the agenda and another to approve the minutes from the previous meeting. The mayor then asks for a motion to approve the consent agenda. The new member proposes moving the item on rescheduling sidewalks from

---

7. Coral B. Ingley and Nicholas T. Van der Walt, "The Strategic Board: The Changing Role of Directors in Developing and Maintaining Corporate Capability," *Corporate Governance* 9, no. 3 (July 2001): 174–85.

8. Svara,"Contributions of the City Council to Effective Governance," 5.

the consent agenda to the regular agenda. The two men she overheard talking before the meeting look at each other and roll their eyes. "Here we go," one murmurs. The other replies, "I told you she was going to cause trouble for us."

The new member considers her situation. "What have I done wrong?" she asks herself. "I wish I had a better sense of the unwritten rules and knew more about how to get things accomplished without alienating others." Scribbling on a notepad, she soon has a long list of questions about how to work with the other members of the council and how to move her issues forward. As she looks at her list, she realizes that she has no clue about where to find answers to her questions. "After the meeting, I'll ask the mayor," she decides.

What should board members consider before implementing an evaluation?

Evaluation can be challenging for any governing board. Evaluation for local government boards in North Carolina is particularly challenging because public boards are bound by open meeting laws and "a discussion of a board's relationship within itself—that is, how the members work together and how they might improve"—must take place in an open session.[9] Members of the board should understand that a board evaluation process presents both benefits and challenges for the governing body. Before initiating an evaluation, board members should weigh the pros and cons of the evaluation process and decide if they are prepared to proceed. Table 2 presents a list of benefits and challenges generated by city and county elected officials attending a program at the UNC School of Government.[10]

Although members may be uncomfortable publicly discussing poor board performance, it is generally no secret when a public governing body is ineffective or even dysfunctional. Intractable governing problems usually extend beyond the actions of any individual member or any particular composition of members on the governing board. Ineffective relationships and mistrust often become ingrained in the culture and ongoing practices, making it difficult for one person or even a group of board members to alter the performance of the board.[11] By engaging in an evaluation of its work, however, a governing board may identify

---

9. David M. Lawrence, *Open Meetings and Local Governments in North Carolina*, 7th ed. (Chapel Hill, N.C.: UNC School of Government, 2008), 27.

10. Results of group discussion during Manager Evaluation and Board Accountability Workshop, UNC School of Government, April 2007.

11. Roger Fisher and Scott Brown, *Getting Together: Building a Relationship That Gets to Yes* (Boston: Houghton Mifflin, 1988), 129.

Table 2. Perceived Pros and Cons of Governing Board Assessment

Pros	Cons
Establishes a common language and shared understanding of what it means to work well as a governing body.	Sheds light on potential problems within the board; opens board up to negative feedback and fear because "People don't like to look in the mirror."
Serves as a tool for focusing discussions on how to improve the governing body's work. Identifies it in order to improve it.	Takes time to design, implement, review, and decide what action to take based on the evaluation results.
Provides a way for governing body to reflect on how well their actions matched their agreements.	Provides little recourse for governing body as a whole if individual members do not abide by agreed-upon norms.
Focuses the governing body's attention on actions that contribute to the local government's mission and goals for the community. Improves services to the community (e.g., more efficient in use of resources; innovative methods of delivery, funding sources).	Puts pressure on governing board members to respond if governance problems are identified. Members risk seeming disingenuous (some will say they support change then avoid doing anything).
Receives direct feedback from citizens.	Board members lack understanding of public.

areas of strength and reaffirm members' commitment to making a difference for the local government and community.

What constitutes an effective board evaluation?

Board evaluations are most effective when they reflect members' perceptions of how they are currently doing and how they would like to perform in the future. They are a process for learning about individual perceptions and communicating the individual perceptions to the group.[12] It is important for the evaluation to focus on how the board operates as a whole, not on the performance or behaviors of individual members. The goal is to develop the board's ability to discuss its shared work and come up with ideas about how to move forward on common goals.

---

12. Diane J. Duca, *Nonprofit Boards: Roles, Responsibilities and Performance* (New York: John Wiley and Sons, Inc., 1996).

Do all board evaluations look alike?

The process and instrument used for a board evaluation will vary depending upon the board's purposes. Any board evaluation needs to assist the governing board in accomplishing its goals, but one board's goals may be quite different from another's. Using an instrument that covers everything the board is responsible for can result in feedback that is too diffuse. A good evaluation asks about things that are important for effective board performance and things that are related to a board's annual goals.

Topics for board evaluation often include the following:

- board member roles and responsibilities,
- working relationships between board members and professional staff,
- citizen engagement,
- community partnerships,
- long-term capital investments,
- organizational performance oversight and monitoring.

Appendix B provides a list of sample board evaluation items.

A board can seek feedback on its performance in a variety of ways. For instance, at the end of each meeting, the board chair or mayor can quickly go around and ask members for feedback about what went well and what could be improved. This type of feedback is useful for specific issues related to how the board operates as a body, but it is likely to focus on incremental changes needed to improve meeting management rather than on long-term goals. In a more traditional board evaluation process, governing board members assess the effectiveness of their board's actions, expectations, and priorities. Even if the evaluation is limited to a few key topics, the assessment will give members an opportunity to discuss issues important to the board's performance.

Which evaluation instrument should be used?

Evaluations are highly subjective and unique to particular organizations. It is unusual for a board to find a ready-made tool that is perfectly suited to its needs. Instead, the board should identify the areas that board members want to assess and review different evaluation items and sample instruments.

In general, it is helpful to use an evaluation instrument that lets people provide two rankings for each item. For each item, members indicate where they want the board to be (perhaps on a scale of one to five) and also rate where the board currently is (using the same scale.) This allows members to see if there are differences among their expectations for the board and to identify differences between current and expected performance. The evaluation can reveal areas of consensus and shared goals, or it can uncover differences in perception and draw attention to areas that need to be addressed. For example, if some people rate communication among board members as "poor" and others rate it as "excellent," the range of scores indicates a difference in members' perspectives and gives the board an opportunity to clarify expectations and suggest ways to improve.

If a governing board is divided or unclear about what type of feedback would be most useful, members can complete a quick-scan evaluation. A quick-scan evaluation covers a wide range of topics at a very high level. If a majority of members agree that an area needs improvement, a more in-depth set of questions can be developed to look at various aspects of board performance. A quick-scan also reveals areas where members disagree about the board's performance. If members' ratings include a wide range of responses (for example, from "strongly disagree" to "strongly agree"), that is an indication that board members do not see the issue in the same way and would benefit from further clarification about expectations for the board in this area. Appendix C presents an example of a quick-scan evaluation.

Who should participate in the board's evaluation?

Board evaluations can be enhanced with input from selected individuals and groups familiar with the responsibilities and working relationships of the board. Without such input, a board may be limited to making only modest changes, leaving major underlying problems and responsibilities unrecognized.[13] The governing board may invite participation from people who routinely observe and are affected by its work, including the manager, clerk, attorney, and department heads. It may also seek input from key external groups, such as advisory boards, business leaders, and informed citizens.

Some boards choose to use an external facilitator to help with the evaluation process. Knowledgeable facilitators can provide examples of evaluation tools, compile information, prepare a neutral report, and ensure that the feedback process is handled in a fair and respectful manner.

---

13. Thomas P. Holland, "Self-Assessment by Nonprofit Boards," *Nonprofit Management and Leadership* 2, no. 1 (Fall 1991): 25–36.

Figure 5. Evaluation Process

Agree on goals

Critique the process

Develop tool

Determine next steps

Complete tool

Discuss feedback

Compile report

What are the steps in board evaluation?

A board's evaluation process needs to be carefully planned before being implemented. Members of the board will be frustrated if the evaluation process is poorly conducted, the evaluation tool is inconsistent with board priorities, or the process puts individual board members on the spot. A successful evaluation process is one that guides the governing board in (1) preparing, planning, and administering the evaluation; (2) discussing the evaluation results and establishing priorities; and (3) acting on the findings. Figure 5 illustrates the steps in an evaluation process.

An effective board evaluation process is one in which

- board members agree on what they will evaluate;
- appropriate measures are included in the evaluation instrument;
- all board members complete an evaluation and submit it to a board chair or other designated neutral person;

- the neutral person compiles a single, summary report including both the average rating and the range of ratings for each item;
- the board sets aside sufficient time to discuss the feedback of the evaluation (note that the results of a board evaluation must be discussed in an open meeting);
- members agree on priorities and action steps;
- there is an opportunity for people to provide feedback on the evaluation process itself.

When and where should the discussion of the evaluation take place?

Before the evaluation process starts, it is important to decide when and where the results of the evaluation will be discussed. There is rarely enough time in a regularly scheduled meeting for the governing board to engage in a thoughtful discussion. The governing board needs to have enough time to reflect on the evaluation feedback and set goals for itself. Orientation or team-building sessions and retreats often provide such an opportunity.

What type of follow-up is necessary?

After the board discusses the evaluation results, members should develop a set of goals for improving performance. Even if board members agree that they are doing well, there are usually opportunities for improvement. Where performance is below expectations, the discussion should focus on what the board can do differently to be more successful moving forward. A guide for an ongoing board improvement process appears in Figure 6.

As a first step, the board should look at its list of goals and select a limited number of areas for improvement. Even under ideal circumstances, it is difficult for boards to improve skills in more than three to five areas at a time, and too many priorities will be overwhelming for the group. Focusing on the issues that a majority of members agree are important will be most likely to yield positive results. The board should then establish measurable and time-bound performance targets for each priority and incorporate these into the annual calendar used to monitor progress.

The next step is to develop an action plan for each priority. Regardless of the plan a board approves, little will happen if members of the board forget to follow through with their plan. One way to make sure the work gets done is to appoint an individual or a subcommittee to champion each change and monitor its progress. Doing so will help ensure that the board stays on track.

Figure 6.   Process for Committing to Ongoing Improvement

Identify Gaps	Set Targets	Monitor
• Prioritize gaps • Rank important issues	• Determine performance standards • Collect relevant information	• Establish a schedule for follow-up • Agree on actions for outcomes

After the evaluation is completed, the board may find it useful to critique the process. Members should be encouraged to suggest improvements, and the board should make note of these for use in future evaluations.

Questions for Discussion

1. What is the purpose of the board's evaluation?

2. Have governing board members outlined what they expect of each other?

3. Who will participate in the review process?

4. Will the governing board use an external facilitator for the evaluation process?

5. When will the board evaluation be scheduled?

6. Where will the evaluation discussion take place?

7. Who will select performance measures to be included in the evaluation tool?

8. Who will be responsible for compiling results into a single report and providing average ratings and ranges for each item?

9. How will we coordinate the board evaluation process with the manager's performance review?

10. How will the board set measurable performance targets and be responsible for monitoring changes in performance?

Appendix A: Practices for Effective Local Government Management

From *The Effective Local Government Manager*, 3rd ed. (pp. 237–39), © copyright 2004 International City/County Management Association, Washington, D.C. Adapted by permission of the publisher.

Note: When administering and scoring this exercise, it is important to take into account the positions of the participants. Varied roles in the organization will lead to varied responses.

Instructions for participants:

1. Read through the nineteen practices below.
2. Mark whether you think the management practice is highly important (H), moderately important (M), or unimportant (L) for your local government.
3. List your six most important (H) and six least important (L) practices.

Instructions for the board:

1. Tally the top priorities for the entire board to see where there are areas of agreement and disagreement on what practices are most important for your local government.
2. Once you have identified a set of priority practices, these can be used in developing a job advertisement and questions for candidates during the interview process.

Six Most Important Practices	Six Least Important Practices

1. STAFF EFFECTIVENESS: Promoting the development and performance of staff and employees throughout the organization (requires knowledge of interpersonal relations; skill in motivation techniques; ability to identify others' strengths and weaknesses).

The following practices contribute to staff effectiveness:

- *Coaching/mentoring.* Providing direction, support, and feedback to enable others to meet their full potential (requires knowledge of feedback techniques; ability to assess performance and identify others' developmental needs).
- *Team leadership.* Facilitating teamwork (requires knowledge of team relations; ability to direct and coordinate group efforts; skill in leadership techniques).
- *Empowerment.* Creating a work environment that encourages responsibility and decision making at all organizational levels (requires skill in sharing authority and removing barriers to creativity).
- *Delegation.* Assigning responsibility to others (requires skill in defining expectations, providing direction and support, and evaluating results).

2. POLICY FACILITATION: Helping elected officials and other community actors identify, work toward, and achieve common goals and objectives (requires knowledge of group dynamics and political behavior; skill in communication, facilitation, and consensus-building techniques; ability to engage others in identifying issues and outcomes). The following practices contribute to policy facilitation:

- *Facilitative leadership.* Building cooperation and consensus among and within diverse groups by helping them identify common goals and act effectively to achieve them; recognizing interdependent relationships and multiple causes of community issues and anticipating the consequences of policy decisions (requires knowledge of community actors and their interrelationships).
- *Facilitating board effectiveness.* Helping elected officials develop a policy agenda that can be implemented effectively and that serves the best interests of the community (requires knowledge of role/authority relationships between elected and appointed officials; skill in responsibly following the lead of others when appropriate; ability to communicate sound information and recommendations).
- *Mediation/negotiation.* Acting as a neutral party in the resolution of policy disputes (requires knowledge of mediation/negotiation principles; skill in mediation/negotiation techniques).

3. FUNCTIONAL AND OPERATIONAL EXPERTISE AND PLANNING (a component of Service Delivery Management): The following practices contribute to functional and operational planning and expertise:

- *Functional/operational expertise.* Understanding the basic principles of service delivery in functional areas—for example, public safety, community and economic development, human and social services, administrative services, public works (requires knowledge of service areas and delivery options).
- *Operational planning.* Anticipating future needs, organizing work operations, and establishing timetables for work units or projects (requires knowledge of technological advances and changing standards; skill in identifying and understanding trends; skill in predicting the impact of service delivery decisions).

4. CITIZEN SERVICE (a component of Service Delivery Management): Determining citizen needs and providing responsive, equitable services to the community (requires skill in assessing community needs and allocating resources; knowledge of information-gathering techniques).

5. PERFORMANCE MEASUREMENT/MANAGEMENT AND QUALITY ASSURANCE (a component of Service Delivery Management): Maintaining a consistently high level of quality in staff work, operational procedures, and service delivery (requires knowledge of organizational processes; ability to facilitate organizational improvements; ability to set performance/productivity standards and objectives and to measure results).

6. INITIATIVE, RISK TAKING, VISION, CREATIVITY, AND INNOVATION (a component of Strategic Leadership): Setting an example that urges the organization and the community toward experimentation, change, creative problem solving, and prompt action (requires knowledge of personal leadership style; skill in visioning, shifting perspectives, and identifying options; ability to create an environment that encourages initiative and innovation). The following practices contribute to initiative, risk taking, vision, creativity, and innovation:

- *Initiative and risk taking.* Demonstrating a personal orientation toward action and accepting responsibility for the results; resisting the status quo, and removing stumbling blocks that delay progress toward goals and objectives.
- *Vision.* Conceptualizing an ideal future state and communicating it to the organization and the community.

- *Creativity and innovation.* Developing new ideas or practices; applying existing ideas and practices to new situations.

7. TECHNOLOGICAL LITERACY (a component of Strategic Leadership): Demonstrating an understanding of information technology and ensuring that it is incorporated appropriately in plans to improve service delivery, information sharing, organizational communication, and citizen access (requires knowledge of technological options and their application).

8. DEMOCRATIC ADVOCACY AND CITIZEN PARTICIPATION: Demonstrating a commitment to democratic principles by respecting elected officials, community interest groups, and the decision making process; educating citizens about local government; and acquiring knowledge of the social, economic, and political history of the community (requires knowledge of democratic principles, political processes, and local government law; skill in group dynamics, communication, and facilitation; ability to appreciate and work with diverse individuals and groups and to follow the community's lead in the democratic process). The following practices contribute to democratic advocacy and citizen participation:

- *Democratic advocacy.* Fostering the values and integrity of representative government and local democracy through action and example; ensuring the effective participation of local government in the intergovernmental system (requires knowledge of and skill in intergovernmental relations).
- *Citizen participation.* Recognizing the right of citizens to influence local decisions and promoting active citizen involvement in local governance.

9. DIVERSITY: Understanding and valuing the differences among individuals and fostering these values throughout the organization and the community.

10. BUDGETING: Preparing and administering the budget (requires knowledge of budgeting principles and practices, revenue sources, projection techniques, and financial control systems; skill in communicating financial information).

11. FINANCIAL ANALYSIS: Interpreting financial information to assess the short-term and long-term fiscal condition of the community, determine the cost-effectiveness of programs, and compare alternative strategies (requires knowledge of analytical techniques and skill in applying them).

12. HUMAN RESOURCES MANAGEMENT: Ensuring that the policies and procedures for employee hiring, promotion, performance appraisal, and discipline are equitable, legal, and current; ensuring that human resources are adequate to accomplish programmatic objectives (requires knowledge of personnel practices and employee relations law; ability to project workforce needs).

13. STRATEGIC PLANNING: Positioning the organization and the community for events and circumstances that are anticipated in the future (requires knowledge of long-range and strategic planning techniques; skill in identifying trends that will affect the community; ability to analyze and facilitate policy choices that will benefit the community in the long run).

14. ADVOCACY AND INTERPERSONAL COMMUNICATION: Facilitating the flow of ideas, information, and understanding between and among individuals; advocating effectively in the community's interest (requires knowledge of interpersonal and group communication principles; skill in listening, speaking, and writing; ability to persuade without diminishing the views of others). The following practices contribute to advocacy and interpersonal communication:

- *Advocacy.* Communicating personal support for policies, programs, or ideals that serve the best interests of the community.
- *Interpersonal communication.* Exchanging verbal and nonverbal messages with others in a way that demonstrates respect for the individual and furthers organizational and community objectives (requires ability to receive verbal and nonverbal cues; skill in selecting the most effective communication method for each interchange).

15. PRESENTATION SKILLS: Conveying ideas or information effectively to others (requires knowledge of presentation techniques and options; ability to match presentation to audience).

16. MEDIA RELATIONS: Communicating information to the media in a way that increases public understanding of local government issues and activities and builds a positive relationship with the press (requires knowledge of media operations and objectives).

17. INTEGRITY: Demonstrating fairness, honesty, and ethical and legal awareness in personal and professional relationships and activities (requires knowledge of business and personal ethics; ability to understand issues of ethics and integrity in specific situations). The following practices contribute to integrity:

- *Personal integrity.* Demonstrating accountability for personal actions; conducting personal relationships and activities fairly and honestly.
- *Professional integrity.* Conducting professional relationships and activities fairly, honestly, legally, and in conformance with the ICMA Code of Ethics (requires knowledge of administrative ethics and specifically the ICMA Code of Ethics).
- *Organizational integrity.* Fostering ethical behavior throughout the organization through personal example, management practices, and training (requires knowledge of administrative ethics; ability to instill accountability into operations; and ability to communicate ethical standards and guidelines to others).

18. PERSONAL DEVELOPMENT: Demonstrating a commitment to a balanced life through ongoing self-renewal and development in order to increase personal capacity (includes maintaining personal health; living by core values; continuous learning and improvement; and creating interdependent relationships and respect for differences).

19. BOARD RELATIONS: Developing and maintaining quality relationships with each member of the governing board and with the board as a whole (requires skills in communication; clear understanding of roles and responsibilities; ability to create trust among the parties; willingness to freely give and receive information).

Appendix B: Sample Board Evaluation Items

Note: These items are drawn from sample evaluations and references on board effectiveness. When selecting items for a board evaluation, it is important to focus on priorities. Try to include no more than thirty items on the evaluation.

Legal and Ethical

Items focus on how members receive information and orientation as well as how they adhere to laws, ethical standards, local policies, and board procedures.

Board Orientation and Information

1. Board members receive a complete orientation and training on their roles and responsibilities.
2. Orientation to the local government includes information about the organization's history, culture, and traditions.
3. The board's and the organization's values are written and everyone knows what they are.
4. Board members understand the local government's mission and how it relates to products and programs.
5. Leaders in this organization go out of their way to make sure all board members have access to the same information.
6. Materials pertaining to significant decisions are given to members in advance of the meetings.
7. Board members arrive prepared for meetings.
8. The board regularly discusses roles and responsibilities and every member fully understands them.

Legal and Ethical Responsibilities

9. The board is legal and respects the spirit as well as the intent of the law in its actions.
10. The governing body reflects a sense of public service over personal interest.
11. Board members are familiar with the freedoms and limitations of their legal status.
12. Board members understand their legal responsibility to the organization.
13. The board understands and accepts responsibility (legal, moral, and ethical) for the actions of all employees in the organization.
14. The organization operates in accordance with its legal authority.
15. The board acts as trustees of the organization on behalf of the community at large.
16. All board members complete ethics certification within one year of being elected.
17. Policies and procedures are in place to deal with ethical issues such as conflicts of interest.

Board Policies and Procedures

18. Governance structures within the board are clear (chair's or mayor's role, committee roles, staff and board roles)
19. Board meetings serve a useful purpose.
20. Board meetings are managed effectively.
21. The board chair or mayor facilitates board discussions.
22. There is a clear protocol for how issues get on the agenda.
23. The board ensures that meeting agendas are structured to keep the focus on priority issues.
24. Agenda items reflect important issues for the organization and community.
25. The governing board provides adequate time for public input at meetings.
26. There is adequate public participation in the selection of committee and advisory board membership.
27. The board pays as much attention to how decisions are made as it does to the final conclusion.
28. The board faithfully discloses information to the public.
29. Governing board policies are communicated effectively.
30. The board has written rules for how it governs the city, town, or county.
31. Board policies are documented and available to every board member.

32. The board has a defined process to identify major changes needed to improve organizational leadership, structures, programs, or resources.

33. The board has an annual calendar of meetings.

34. The board has a process for handling urgent matters between meetings.

Working with Others

Items focus on how board members interact with one another, professional staff, and community stakeholders.

Interactions on the Board

35. When a new member joins the board, someone serves as a mentor to help the person learn the ropes.

36. The board cultivates leadership among its members.

37. Relationships among board members are characterized by openness, trust, and mutual respect.

38. When conflicts arise, they are generally acknowledged and dealt with in an open, positive manner.

39. Adequate time and energy is devoted to getting every board member's input.

40. The board often requests that a decision be postponed until more information is available.

41. Disagreements are more often resolved by discussion than by a vote.

42. Board members try to reach consensus.

43. Individual governing board members avoid unduly consuming meeting time.

44. Board members are attuned to the subtleties of issues.

45. The board operates as an effective team.

46. Board members have common expectations about behavior.

47. Board members communicate openly with each other.

48. Board members feel safe expressing controversial views.

49. Governing board members avoid over-politicizing the public process.

50. The organization succeeds because of the contributions and leadership of many people rather than a few.

51. The board recognizes special events in the lives of its members.

52. It is rewarding to be a part of the board.

Interactions with Staff

53. Relationships among board members, the public manager, and staff are characterized by openness, trust, and mutual respect.

54. The organization attracts and retains competent and motivated people.

55. Members of the board and senior staff are comfortable managing change.

56. The board and staff work as a team to plan and manage change.

57. Board members behave in a respectful manner toward staff.

58. The board understands and respects the norms of the professional staff working for the organization.

59. Board members view staff as trusted partners.

60. The governing board, as a unit, gives direction to the professional staff.

61. The governing body gives adequate consideration to staff recommendations.

62. The staff has adequate opportunity to participate in the governing board's meetings.

63. Training and development opportunities for staff are included in the annual budget.

64. The board periodically requests information on the morale of the professional staff.

65. The board delegates operation of the local government to the manager.

66. Board members view the public manager as a credible, professional leader.

67. Roles and expectations of the public manager are clearly defined and communicated.

68. The public manager has an opportunity to provide input during the decision-making process.

69. There is an open and honest relationship between the governing board and the public manager.

70. There is mutual respect between the governing board and the public manager.

71. The organization has committees that include professional staff and board members.

72. There is at least as much dialogue between board members as there is between members and management.

Interactions with Stakeholders

73. The local government works effectively with other organizations, businesses, and groups in the community.

74. This board seeks information and advice from leaders of similar and related organizations.

75. The board listens to stakeholders with diverse views, opinions, and experiences.

76. Relationships among board members and the public are characterized by openness, trust, and mutual respect.

77. If the board thinks a key constituency or stakeholder group may disagree with an issue it is considering, it will make an effort to hear from the group directly before taking action.

78. Board members are active and effective in representing the community's interests.

79. The board appoints citizens, staff members, and other stakeholders as appropriate to committees and advisory boards.

80. Advisory committee membership is based on the ability to serve the community rather than on personal friendships.

81. The board gives sufficient weight and attention to recommendations of advisory committees.

Making Decisions and Setting Direction

Items address the board's responsibility to set goals, clarify values and priorities, and maintain a long-term vision for the organization and the community.

Quality Decision Making

82. Board decisions are innovative.

83. The governing board is able to make hard choices and politically unpopular decisions when necessary.

84. The board does not attempt to avoid issues that are ambiguous or complicated.

85. The board examines the pros and cons of decisions it is about to make.

86. When faced with a complex issue, the board often brainstorms to generate a list of creative options or solutions.

87. All of the board's decisions relate to its mission.

88. The board makes every effort to take action before an issue becomes urgent or critical.

Developing Goals, Priorities, and Long-Term Vision

89. The local government's vision, mission, and values drive the decisions and choices the board makes.

90. The board has a common vision and shared goals.

91. The board's roles, such as focusing on policy and long-term planning, are defined and respected.

92. The board and staff have a systematic process for setting strategic goals and objectives that reflect their mission and vision for the future.

93. The board sets the right balance between long-term vision and immediate needs.

94. The board considers the long-term planning priorities of the organization when dealing with policy issues.

95. Goals established by the board are realistic and doable within the time frame stated.

96. At least once a year, the board asks the public manager to articulate his or her vision for the future and strategies for achieving it.

Linking the Organization to the Community

97. Board meetings focus on important community matters.

98. The board discusses events and trends in the larger environment that may present opportunities or challenges for the local government and community.

99. The organization incorporates change into its planning process.

100. The board spends time discussing issues of importance to the community's future.

101. This board often discusses where the local government and community should be in five or ten years.

Providing Resources

Items address the board's oversight and allocation of resources to achieve organizational goals and priorities.

102. The board takes a lead role in setting expectations for financial management.

103. The board ensures that adequate financial tools and resources are in place for the organization to accomplish strategic objectives.

104. The board is responsible for ensuring that finances are closely related to performance expectations and the local government's mission.

105. The governing board understands the local government's financial resources and makes sound decisions to prioritize spending.

106. The board has clear financial policies and procedures in place.

107. The board has a long term-financial plan.

108. The board has a policy for handling adjustments and revisions to the budget.

109. The board avoids unbudgeted appropriations.

110. The board avoids changing the budget after its adoption except in emergencies or to handle unforeseen situations.

111. The board approves specific targets and limits on things such as debt, liquidity, and other financial ratios to warn of poor financial performance.

112. The board makes sure that the organization has the necessary tools and resources in place to manage its employees.

113. The board supports professional development for the public manager and employees.

114. Costs and benefits of services are analyzed and provided to the community and service users.

Accountability

Items relate to how the board maintains transparency, responsiveness, and accountability.

Accountability to the Public

115. Board members effectively represent the organization in community settings.

116. The public is adequately informed about the governing board's goals.

117. The board engages people from within the organization as well as outside to address the needs of citizens.

118. There is adequate opportunity for a cross section of the public to participate in the budget process.

119. The board regularly seeks feedback from a wide range of community members on the quality and effectiveness of the services they receive.

120. The local government's mission, vision, and values are reflected in the organization's reports, publications, and website.

Accountability to the Organization

121. The board receives regular (monthly or quarterly) reports on finance/budget and program performance.
122. The board reviews financial statements of expenditures and revenues against an approved budget monthly.
123. The board regularly reviews and discusses reports that provide performance data on programs and services, using comparable performance data where available.
124. The board regularly evaluates organization's services and activities.
125. The board understands its responsibilities as an employer.
126. The board provides annual feedback on the public manager's performance.
127. The board's policies fairly compensate the public manager for good performance.
128. The governing board considers the impact of changing priorities on staff time.
129. The whole organization continuously challenges itself to improve.

Accountability as a Board

130. The board has adopted explicit goals for itself that are distinct from the goals for the organization.
131. Governing board members participate in implementing goals once they are established.
132. The board regularly monitors and evaluates progress toward strategic goals and program performance.
133. The board establishes reasonable time frames for accomplishing assignments.
134. Recommendations from evaluations and feedback are used for planning and performance improvement.
135. The board has a retreat or special session at least every two years that includes a discussion of the board's performance and how well it is governing.
136. The board acknowledges its responsibility for poor decisions.

Sources Used in Compiling List of Board Evaluation Items—All Useful References for Governing Boards

Barrett, Katherine, and Richard Greene. "Short on Oversight." *Governing* (May 2006): 80.

Brown, William A. "Exploring the Association between Board and Organizational Performance in Nonprofit Organizations." *Nonprofit Management and Leadership* 15, no. 3 (Spring 2005): 317–39.

Duca, Diane J. *Nonprofit Boards: Roles, Responsibilities and Performance.* New York: John Wiley and Sons, Inc., 1996.

Dunn, Delmer D., and Jerome S. Legge Jr. "Accountability and Responsibility of Local Government Administrators." In *The Future of Local Government Administration.* Edited by H. George Frederickson and John Nalbandian. Washington, D.C.: International City/County Management Association, 2002.

Fisher, Roger, and Scott Brown. *Getting Together: Building Relationships as We Negotiate.* Boston: Houghton Mifflin, 1988.

Fisher, Roger, and Daniel Shapiro. *Beyond Reason.* London: Penguin, 2005.

Gabris, G. T., and K. L. Nelson. "Transforming Municipal Boards into Accountable, High-Performing Teams: Toward a Diagnostic Model of Governing Board Effectiveness." *Public Performance and Management Review*, 36, no. 3 (March 2013): 472–95.

Herman, Robert D., and David O. Renz, "Board Practices of Especially Effective and Less Effective Local Nonprofit Organizations." *American Review of Public Administration* 30, no. 2 (June 2000): 146–60.

Holland, Thomas P. "Self-Assessment by Nonprofit Boards." *Nonprofit Management and Leadership* 2, no. 1 (Fall 1991): 25–36.

Ingley, Coral B., and Nicholas T. Van der Walt. "The Strategic Board: The Changing Role of Directors in Developing and Maintaining Corporate Capability." *Corporate Governance* 9, no. 3 (July 2001): 174–85.

Jenne, Kurt. "County Management." Chap. 2 in *County Government in North Carolina*, 4th ed. Edited by A. Fleming Bell and Warren Jake Wicker. Chapel Hill, N.C.: UNC Institute of Government, 1998.

Lawrence, David M. *Open Meetings and Local Governments in North Carolina*, 7th ed. Chapel Hill, NC: UNC School of Government, 2008.

Newell, Charldean. "Enhancing the Governing Body's Effectiveness." Chap. 3 in *The Effective Local Government Manager*. Washington, D.C.: International City/County Management Association, 2004.

Newell, Charldean, ed. *The Effective Local Government Manager*. Washington, D.C.: International City/County Management Association, 2004.

Schwarz, Roger et al. *The Skilled Facilitator Fieldbook*. San Francisco: Jossy-Bass, 2005.

Svara, James H. "Contributions of the City Council to Effective Governance." *Popular Government* 51, no. 4 (Spring 1986).

Tomey, Edward J. *Nonprofit Board Self-Assessment Guidebook*. Keene, N.H.: Antioch University New England, 1995.

UNC School of Government, "An Effective Council (Operating Principles)," www.sog.unc.edu/sites/www.sog.unc.edu/files/An%20Effective%20Council.pdf.

Walker, Larry W. "Governing Board, Know Thyself: Self-Assessment Is the Basis for High Performance." *Trustee* 52, no. 8 (September 1999): 15–19.

Wilson, S. Leigh, Fred P. Baggett, and Warren Jake Wicker. "Governance in Mayor-Council Cities." Chap. 5 in *Municipal Government in North Carolina*, 2nd ed. Chapel Hill, NC: UNC Institute of Government, 1995.

Appendix C: Governing Board Quick-Scan

Use this Governing Board Quick-Scan to identify your board's strengths and areas for improvement in preparation for a more in-depth board evaluation. This instrument is not intended to serve as a substitute for a full board evaluation but rather to help the board determine what issues members feel need attention.

Scoring Key:
SD (Strongly Disagree)=1   **D** (Disagree)=2   **A** (Agree)=3   **SA** (Strongly Agree)=4

Governing Board Quick-Scan	SD	D	A	SA
Board members receive a complete orientation and training on their roles and responsibilities.	1	2	3	4
Board members operate within their legal authority.	1	2	3	4
Board members demonstrate commitment to this organization's mission and values.	1	2	3	4
This board has a systematic process for setting strategic goals and objectives that reflect our mission and vision for the future.	1	2	3	4
This board's ability to govern effectively is not impaired by conflict among its members.	1	2	3	4
This board's meetings are well managed.	1	2	3	4
This board uses sound decision-making methods (focused on board-level issues, factual information, efficient use of time, effective implementation).	1	2	3	4
This board has adopted explicit goals for itself that are distinct from the goals for the organization.	1	2	3	4
All board members can distinguish between and respect their own and the manager's roles and responsibilities.	1	2	3	4

(continued)

Governing Board Quick-Scan	SD	D	A	SA
There is a productive working relationship (good communication and mutual respect) between members of the board and the organization's manager.	1	2	3	4
The board makes sure that adequate financial resources are in place for the organization to be viable and stable and accomplish strategic objectives.	1	2	3	4
This board does a good job evaluating the performance of the manager (measuring results based on clear objectives).	1	2	3	4
This board could effectively manage any organizational crisis that might reasonably be anticipated.	1	2	3	4
This board and organization have a good balance between organizational stability and innovation.	1	2	3	4
This board has high credibility with key stakeholders (voters, community leaders, staff, and partner organizations).	1	2	3	4
Column Totals				
Total for all 15 items				
Overall Score (Total divided by 15)				

www.ingramcontent.com/pod-product-compliance
Lightning Source LLC
Chambersburg PA
CBHW080244270326
41926CB00020B/4370